Breaking Barriers

Overcoming Communication Challenges in Relationships

Table of Contents

Chapter 1. Introduction

Introducing our Special Report: "Breaking Barriers: Overcoming Communication Challenges in Relationships". In the labyrinth of love and togetherness, we often find ourselves at crossroads due to communication hurdles, don't we? This engaging report takes you on a compelling journey to discover the secrets of effective relationship communication. Packed with real-life case studies, expert insights, practical strategies and exciting communication exercises, this report is a golden ticket to a world where love and understanding hold the reins. Can't you already feel the walls coming down? Buckle up, for you are about to embark on an adventurous voyage towards breaking barriers and building bridges in your relationship! Let this introductory paragraph not merely be an invitation, but the first step towards a powerful transformation. Trust us, this is the best thing you'll buy today! You can thank us later.

Chapter 2. Understanding the Role of Communication in Relationships

Communication, in its various forms, serves as the cement that holds relationships together. But what happens when the concept of communication itself becomes shadowy? Well, misunderstandings creep in, causing friction in relationships. This chapter delves into the profound role of communication in relationships, allowing us to explore its intricacies and influence.

2.1. Communication: The Bedrock of Relationships

At its core, communication in relationships is about conveying messages and understanding the sentiments of each other. Every relationship, whether it be romantic, platonic, familial, or professional, relies heavily on this crucial element. It serves as a medium to express feelings, share experiences, and navigate through disagreements productively.

One of the principal powers of communication lies in fostering understanding. It holds the potential to illuminate and clarify, helping us delve into the mindsets, intentions, and emotions of our counterparts. A slight misunderstanding can trigger a cascade of complications, but clear communication can pave the way to a smoother journey.

2.2. Types of Communication in Relationships

A relationship can contain various types of communication, each playing an essential role, including verbal, non-verbal, and even written communication.

Verbal Communication

Verbal communication essentially involves using words to express oneself. It can range from casual, everyday conversations to weighty emotional topics. Yet, how we converse leaves a substantial impact on our relationships. A study by Robnett and Leaper (2013) revealed that comforting words and using terms of endearment strengthened romantic bonds.

Non-Verbal Communication

Non-verbal communication, on the other hand, includes facial expressions, body language, and tone of voice. According to Dr. Albert Mehrabian's 7-38-55 Rule, these non-verbal elements make up the majority of our communication (Mehrabian, 1971). While words might fail us or even deceive the listener, the body language and tone never lie.

Written Communication

Lastly, written communication while often overlooked, is another vital part of our interactions. Letters, text messages, emails, notes—all form part of written communication. In a digital age, where long-distance relationships are increasingly common, the importance of effective written communication can't be overstated.

2.3. The Role of Active Listening in Communication

Listening doesn't merely mean hearing the words that the other person is saying. It's about understanding their emotions, empathizing with them, and responding appropriately. This is called active listening, a powerful tool for building mutual understanding and trust.

Our relationships would enrich significantly if we imbibe this knack of active listening. When one person genuinely listens, the other feels valued and acknowledged, creating a positive cycle that bolsters connection and intimacy in the relationship.

2.4. The Impact of Poor Communication in Relationships

Lack of effective communication can profoundly impact relationships, manifesting as misunderstandings, hurt feelings, and, gradually, mistrust. Over time, these negative outcomes can damage, or even spell the end of, relationships.

Gottman's Four Horsemen theory of relationship downfall (criticism, contempt, defensiveness, and stonewalling) is seated deeply in poor communication (Gottman, 1999). This theory demonstrates the vicious cycle that poor communication often results in, leading to long term damage.

2.5. Building Constructive Communication Habits

To foster healthier interactions and avoid the pitfalls of ineffective communication, there is a need to develop good communication habits. Including clear expression, emotional honesty, respectful disagreements, maintaining eye contact, keeping an open mind, and using "I" statements instead of "you" statements.

These habits help in bridging the communication gap making one feel heard, validated, and loved. Constructive communication can turn the tide of both personal romantic and platonic relationships and professional ones.

This chapter offers us a playground to understand the role communication plays in our relationships. Fathoming this can lead us to fewer misconceptions, less conflict, and more relational happiness. It's of utmost importance to remember that while it might feel difficult initially, changing our communication patterns can lead to profound impacts on our relationships. Both the journey and the destination promise to be incredibly satisfying. One must not disregard the powerful role clear, open communication can have in transforming our relationships.

As we conclude this chapter, we implore you to practice the strategies discussed and experienced the transformative power of effective communication. Remember, the path to great relationships often starts by mastering the art of communication!

(References)

Gottman, J. M. (1999). The marriage clinic: A scientifically based marital therapy. WW Norton & Company.

Mehrabian, A. (1971). Silent messages. Wadsworth.

Robnett, R. D., & Leaper, C. (2013). Friendship groups, personal motivation, and gender in relation: Predictors of prospective science motivation. Journal of Research on Adolescence, 23(2), 263–273.

Chapter 3. Mirror, Mirror on the Wall: Self-reflection in Communication

When one steps in front of a mirror, they don't just see a simple reflection. Instead, they come face-to-face with their deepest thoughts, emotions, fears, strengths, weaknesses, and aspirations. Self-reflection in communication shares a strikingly similar concept. It's akin to holding a mirror to oneself, to intimately understand our ways of communicating, to identify areas of improvement, and to align our communication with our intent and values.

3.1. The Essence of Self-Reflection

Self-reflection is the process of paying conscious attention to your thoughts, emotions, decisions, behaviors, and overall ways of seeing and interacting with the world. It enables you to make sense of your actions, to learn and develop from experiences, and to gain a greater understanding of yourself and of those around you.

In communication, self-reflection involves observing and analyzing how one expresses themselves, responds to others, manages emotions, and behaves in different contexts and relationships. It's about understanding your own communication patterns, while also identifying the impact of these patterns on your interactions, relationships, and your self-concept.

3.2. Understanding Self-reflection in Communication: The What and the Why

Self-reflection in communication is not merely thinking about what you said or did in a specific situation. Rather, it's about delving deeper and asking yourself why you chose certain words, why you reacted in a particular way, or why you felt certain emotions. It's about connecting these answers to your personal beliefs, values, assumptions, attitudes, and emotional needs.

Reflecting on your communication is not an easy task—it requires honesty, courage, openness, and a willingness to learn and change. Nonetheless, it's crucial for several reasons. It allows you to gain clarity about your communication issues, to identify non-constructive communication habits, to foster greater empathy and understanding, and to improve your ability to express, connect, and build meaningful relationships.

3.3. The Process of Self-Reflection in Communication

Self-reflection in communication is a multi-step process, which involves:

1. Awareness: The first step involves developing an awareness of your communication style, tendencies, strengths, and areas of improvement. You can cultivate this awareness by paying attention to your interactions, noticing your body language, listening to your tone of voice, observing your emotional reactions, and understanding the content, context, and consequences of your messages.

2. Evaluation: In the second step, you objectively analyze your

communication. Did it match your intentions? Did you express your thoughts and feelings effectively? Were you listening and responding emphatically? Were you being respectful and considerate? Did your non-verbals align with your verbal message?

3. Insight and Learning: Here, you extract lessons from your evaluation. What can you learn from your successes and mistakes? What patterns do you notice? What insights can you gather about your communication and yourself?

4. Planning and Change: Finally, based on your insights, you plan and implement changes. You practice new behaviors, experiment with different communication strategies, and assess the impact of these changes on your interactions and relationships.

3.4. The Role of Self-Reflection in Conflict Resolution

Often, conflicts arise and escalate because we react without understanding. We misinterpret signals, we let our assumptions and biases take over, we let our emotions dominate our words. Self-reflection can help us manage and resolve conflicts more effectively by providing us with the tools to understand both our and the other's perspectives.

When we reflect, we can explore our emotional triggers, understand our role in the conflict, recognize the deeper issues at play, and develop more insightful responses. As such, self-reflection allows us to shift from a reactive to a more thoughtful, understanding, and empathic communication mode, paving the way for constructive conflict resolution.

3.5. Tips for Enhancing Self-Reflection in Communication

Improving your self-reflection in communication requires continuous effort. Some tips to guide you in this journey include: Staying open-minded, asking for feedback, keeping a communication diary, practicing mindfulness, and engaging in regular self-reflection exercises. Each of these steps will act as a building block towards enhancing your communication skills, your interpersonal relationships, and your personal growth.

Remember, just like gazing into a mirror, self-reflection can reveal things you might not have noticed before. It might be uncomfortable at times, but it is also enlightening. Being dedicated to reflection will surely lead to enriching discoveries and improvements in how you connect and communicate with the world around you.

So, go ahead, hold up that mirror, and embark on this enlightening journey to deeper self-awareness, and in turn, a more profound and rewarding connection with others. The path may seem arduous, but rest assured, the rewards of mastering effective communication are truly infinite.

Chapter 4. When Silence Speaks: Decoding Unspoken Words

Communication is a complex dance that goes beyond the spoken word. The vaudeville of words is but a single melodious note in the symphony of effective communication. There exists a far more profound, yet often ignored realm — the kingdom of silence. Amid the hustle and bustle of everyday conversations, we often overlook the potent messages residing within the silences. But how can we decipher these unvocalized emotions, the labyrinth of thoughts not externalized, the sentiments left unexpressed? This exploration of silence as a form of communication aims to illuminate this landscape.

4.1. The Power of Silence

Often in relationships, one might encounter a partner's silence as a response. The silent treatment could imply resentment, disapproval, or disagreement. Simultaneously, it can also signify contentment or a thoughtful moment, each silence possessing its individuality.

Even in the absence of verbal expression, our emotions tend to surface subtly via body language, facial expressions or energy. This silent communication often includes nuances that words fail to capture. Seasoned relationships understand the difference in silences: a comforting quietude from a stinging silence.

Let's turn towards body language – the silent spokesperson of our inner world. To master decoding unspoken words, we must first comprehend the language of the body. In the following sections, we will examine different forms of body language that act as windows to unexpressed emotions and unsaid words.

4.2. Understanding Body Language

Body language, a form of non-verbal communication, involves conscious or unconscious body actions and gestures. Primarily, it includes eye movements, facial expressions, posture, and other physical gestures.

1. Eye Movement: The eyes are the mirror of the soul; they seldom lie. A glance can expose an array of emotions – fear, love, disgust, surprise, and more. Prolonged eye contact can reveal confidence or attraction, while averted eyes might signal discomfort or deceit.

2. Facial Expressions: Facial expressions, nearly universal, largely remain involuntary. A smile, a frown, a twitch, each deliver discrete messages about our emotional state.

3. Posture: The way we carry ourselves communicates our attitude. An upright posture may signify confidence, while slumped shoulders could denote low self-esteem or disappointment.

4. Physical Touch: Touch is extremely personal and subjective. A gentle touch can express affection, encouragement, or consolation, while aggressive or harsh touch could imply dominance or displeasure.

The meticulous observation and interpretation of these cues form the crux of comprehending the silent language.

4.3. The Science Behind Silence

Comprehending silence involves neuroscience principles as our brains are wired to pick up those subtle signals. Our prefrontal cortex analyzes and decodes these emotional cues so we can respond appropriately. This neural alchemy, in a split second, solves the cryptic puzzle of silent communication.

Indeed, silence is a language spoken by everyone but understood only by those fluent in their observation.

Several scientific studies have deliberated over silence and its implications on human disposition. The power of silence, under proven circumstances, fosters a greater depth of empathy and understanding. Occupying the vast expanse between two words, silence provides room for coherent understanding and emotional connections to flourish.

4.4. The Art of Active Listening

Active listening is a vital skill in decoding silent communication. This involves paying full attention to the speaker, showing a genuine interest, and providing feedback. When your partner goes silent, active listening enables you to decipher the message enveloped within, contributing to a comprehensive understanding of their emotional grounding.

Building on this, we can conclude that silence is not the absence of communication, but a unique, potent signal in its own right. The trick lies in tuning in to listen to its delicate whispers.

4.5. The Practice of Silence Analysis

To decode silence, one needs practice, patience, and a profound understanding of the partner's behavioral patterns. Here are some pointers:

1. Empathy: Understand the emotions behind the silence.

2. Observation: Watch for nonverbal cues.

3. Patience: Give your partner the space they require; haste can lead to misinterpretation.

4. Respect: Respect the silence as you would respect spoken words.

Decode the unsaid, understand the unspoken, and embark on your voyage into the silent echoes of the heart.

When decoded properly, silence speaks volumes. It serves as a foundation for compassion and mutual understanding. Remember, in the world of unspoken messages, silence is not empty; it's full of answers. So, heed the silence, for it often yells out what words fail to whisper. Now, equipped with these insights, you can venture into communicating more efficiently, thereby nurturing healthier and more fulfilling relationships. The barriers of misunderstanding have begun to crumble, making way for a world where empathy, patience, and silence reign supreme!

Chapter 5. The Art of Active Listening: More Than Just Hearing

Active listening is a bedrock of effective communication in a relationship. It transcends hearing, creating an atmosphere where our partners feel valued, heard, and understood. This process involves more than just the auditory sense; it encapsulates body language, emotional cues, and an empathetic mindset. Active listening is the key to unlocking a deeper level of connection, promoting shared understanding and driving meaningful conversations.

5.1. Understanding Active Listening

Active listening is predicated upon the intentional focus on the speaker and their message. This receptive orientation involves a complete immersion into the speaker's world in order to grasp their viewpoint completely. Any other distracting thoughts are put aside. Active listening is not about you, the listener. It's about those to whom you're listening.

5.2. The Disconnect: Hearing vs. Listening

Hearing is a passive process that requires minimal effort. While listening, we unconsciously pick up sounds and may sometimes catch fragments of information. The process is involuntary and requires no willpower or engagement on our part.

On the other hand, listening is a voluntary process that requires conscious work. It involves not only hearing the message but understanding and interpreting it too. Listening is the endeavor of decoding the speaker's underlying emotions, intentions, and unspoken words.

5.3. Components of Active Listening

Active listening is constituted by several major elements:

1. Attentiveness: Our focus should remain on the speaker, paying greater heed to their words over our thoughts or responses.

2. Body Language: Non-verbal cues are powerful indicators of how attentively we're listening. Maintain eye contact and use open body language to show you're engaged.

3. Feedback: Confirm your understanding by summarizing the points made by the speaker and asking clarification questions.

4. Empathy: Understand the speaker's emotions and respond appropriately.

5. Patience: Listen entirely before formulating your response.

5.4. The Power of Non-Verbal Communication

Non-verbal cues including eye contact, facial expressions, and gestures are the unsaid words with their immense capability of expressing emotions. They bridge the gap where words fail. As a listener, be aware of these cues, they add constructs to the speaker's narrative, manifesting their emotions accurately.

5.5. The Art of Responding

Enriched by the speaker's perspective, your responses should reflect comprehension and empathy. Responsiveness should not merely be an articulation of your opinions or advice. It is a powerful tool for validating the speaker's emotions and crystallizing their perspective.

5.6. Roadblocks to Active Listening

Despite its significance, active listening is often hindered by barriers like:

1. Preconceived notions: Entering a conversation with an expectation or biased understanding limits the ability to listen actively.

2. Interrupting: Frequently interrupting a speaker not only conveys disrespect but also disrupts the flow of conversation.

3. Multi-tasking: The flagbearer of inattentiveness, dividing focus invariably cripples the quality of listening.

5.7. Overcoming the Roadblocks

Adopting certain strategies may help overcome these roadblocks:

1. Approach Listen with an Open Mind: Empty your cup of biases before entering a conversation. Being prepared to accept new viewpoints facilitates active listening.

2. Practice Patience: Give the speaker an uninterrupted platform to express themselves.

3. Monotask: Dedicate your entire focus to the conversation. Put aside all potential distractions – physical or mental.

5.8. Real Life Examples

Analyzing real-life scenarios, we find multitudinous instances of active listening aiding in the resolution of conflicts and fostering understanding. Often, issues that seem intractable find resolution when individuals sincerely attempt to listen and understand the other's perspective.

5.9. Active Listening Exercise

Practicing active listening exercises can significantly improve your listening skills in relationships. Next time you engage in a conversation, meticulously extrapolate these steps to practice active listening:

1. Share a Scenario: One partner shares a scenario or experiences;

2. No Interruptions: The other listens conscientiously, withholding any interruption;

3. Reflect: Once done, the listener reflects upon the conveyed message, ensuring their understanding aligns with the speaker's intention;

4. Swap Roles: Swap roles and repeat the exercise.

5.10. Wrapping It Up

Truly, active listening is much more than just sensory input; it entails understanding, emotional engagement, and building fruitful discussions. It is a transformative tool in relationships that cuts through miscommunication, promoting genuine understanding and mutual respect. Practicing active listening is one significant stride towards breaking communication barriers.

Chapter 6. Emotional Intelligence: The Heart of Relationship Communication

Emotional intelligence, often abbreviated as EQ (Emotional Quotient), is a critical factor in maintaining successful relationships. It is the ability to perceive, process, and manage your own emotions along with those of others in a positive and effective way. It is the backbone of better communication, empathy, and interpersonal effectiveness.

6.1. Understanding Emotional Intelligence

Emotional intelligence begins with what we call self-awareness. Many people go through life reacting to events and external stimuli based on conditioned responses, with little conscious thought given to why they react as they do. By understanding our emotions, we can recognize and appreciate why we feel a certain way and take that into account when deciding how to communicate or behave.

Increased self-awareness can also lead to better understanding of others. This is sometimes termed empathy or emotional literacy - the ability to "read" the moods or feelings of others. This can prove to be a vital skill in all forms of relationships, as understanding someone else's perspective can help to avoid conflict and improve communication.

6.2. The Four Components of Emotional Intelligence

Daniel Goleman, a renowned psychologist and author, categorized emotional intelligence into four domains:

1. Self-Awareness: Recognizing your own emotions and how they can affect your thoughts and behavior.

2. Self-Management: Controlling impulsive feelings and behaviors, managing emotions in healthy ways, taking initiative, following through on commitments, and adapting to change.

3. Social Awareness: Understanding the emotions, needs, and concerns of other people.

4. Relationship Management: Knowing how to develop and maintain good relationships, communicate clearly, inspire and influence others, work well in a team, and manage conflict.

6.3. The Role Of Emotional Intelligence In Relationship Communication

Emotionally intelligent people are skilled communicators. They can clearly express their needs and listen to the needs of others, which promotes mutual understanding and respect. They can manage their emotions during heated conversations, thereby being able to avoid verbally attacking their partner or acting defensively.

Emotionally intelligent people are also more likely to value and respect their partner's perspective, even if they disagree. This understanding leads to healthier, more balanced dialogues and can prevent fights from escalating unnecessarily. Emotional intelligence, by fostering effective communication and mutual respect, sets the stage for relationship success.

6.4. Enhancing Emotional Intelligence through Emotional Literacy

Emotional literacy is a key component of emotional intelligence, and it's an ability that can be cultivated and enhanced. Generally, it encompasses two areas:

1. Emotional Identification: Learning to identify and name your feelings is the first step towards emotional literacy. It helps in providing a deeper understanding of your emotions so you can better manage them.

2. Emotional Expression: Expressing emotions in a healthy and constructive way is critical. Bottling up emotions can lead to confusion, misunderstandings, or even resentment in relationships.

6.5. Communicating Better with Emotional Intelligence

To communicate more effectively using emotional intelligence, you can use a few key strategies:

1. Practice Active Listening: Active listening involves completely focusing on your partner's words, refraining from interruptive reactions, and responding thoughtfully. It's a way of showing respect for your partner's feelings and thoughts, which fosters better connection in the relationship.

2. Use 'I' Statements: Instead of blaming your partner (e.g., "You always forget to..."), express how their actions impact you ("I feel

upset when..."). This approach encourages a more constructive, less confrontational conversation.

3. Show Empathy: Try to understand your partner's perspective even if you disagree. This empathy can help them feel heard, valued, and supported.

4. Know When to Pause: If a conversation becomes too heated, take a break to cool down and gather your thoughts. Return to the discussion when both of you are calm and collected.

Emotional intelligence is like a muscle that can be developed over time. Investing energy into nurturing this competence can have powerful effects on the quality of your relationships and the effectiveness of your communication. Remember that with patience, openness, and continual practice, you can significantly improve your emotional intelligence, leading to deeper connections and more satisfying personal relationships.

Chapter 7. Fight Fair: Conflict Management and Resolution

Understanding the complexity of conflicts, how they emerge and evolve, is critical to effective conflict management and resolution in relationships. It's far from simple: it involves knowing the dynamics of an argument, recognizing the role emotions play, appreciating the art of stepping back, and practicing empathy and mutual respect. With the right approach, conflicts can be used as stepping-stones to understanding, intimacy, and stronger partnership.

7.1. The Anatomy of Conflict

All conflicts aren't created equal. They vary significantly in their causes, implications, and how they should be managed. Some conflicts stem from conflicting interests or wants. Others originate in differing worldviews or perceptions, with parties failing to see situations from the same perspective. Yet still, more conflicts arise from incompatible expectations or needs not being met.

Conflicts can be triggered by external factors such as stress, fatigue, or interference from third parties. Internal factors, such as past trauma, emotional instability or certain personality traits, can also light the fuse. Identifying the root cause of a conflict is essential to unravel it and prevent similar issues in the future.

7.2. Emotions in Conflicts

Emotions and their management play a key role in conflict resolution. Amidst a heated argument, intense emotions can overshadow reason, leading to reactive rather than thoughtful responses. Identifying and slowing down emotional reactivity can provide the space needed for a more constructive approach to conflict.

7.3. Skillful Communication in Conflicts

Communication is at the heart of conflict resolution. Active listening, emotional intelligence, assertiveness, patience, and nonverbal communication skills are all paramount. Stay curious about your partner's perspective, actively listen to understand, express your thoughts and feelings assertively but respectfully, and become conscious of your nonverbal cues.

7.4. Harnessing the Power of Empathy

Empathy—the ability to understand and share the feelings of another—is a powerful tool in conflict resolution. It seeks to bridge the gap of misunderstanding and creates an environment of shared humanity, regardless of differing perspectives.

7.5. The Win-Win Mindset

A win-win mindset goes a long way in making conflict resolution constructive. Rather than viewing an argument as a battlefield demanding victory, see it as a problem you and your partner are collaboratively solving.

7.6. Timing and Setting in Conflict Resolution

Recognizing the right time and place to sort out the discord helps maintain dignity and respect. Conflicts often escalate when broached abruptly or in unsuitable settings. Try to engage in conflict resolution discussions when both partners are calm and not distracted.

7.7. The Art of Stepping Back

Sometimes, stepping back offers the best way forward. When conflicts escalate, taking a breather and revisiting the issue later can bring clarity and prevent regrettable actions.

7.8. Repair Attempts

Repair attempts are proactive efforts to deescalate, make peace, and repair the relationship during or after a conflict. Whether it's a pat on the back, a funny comment, or a soft, affectionate tone, these small measures can diffuse tension and foster connection.

7.9. Professional Help

For recurring conflict patterns or escalated cases that prove challenging to manage independently, couples therapy or mediation can provide the necessary guidance and support.

Practical exercises, reflective questions, and self-assessment tools are peppered throughout this chapter to help readers recognize their conflict patterns, improve their communication, and build a stronger, conflict-resilient relationship. The art of conflict resolution may not come easy, but with consistent practice and patience, anyone can master it.

Chapter 8. Bridge Over Troubled Water: Rebuilding Communication After a Fall Out

Navigating the stormy seas of miscommunication and misunderstanding can be a taxing task. Recovering from a fallout requires patience, acceptance, understanding, and most importantly, the willingness to reconnect. Let's delve deep and lay out the roadmap to rebuilding the bridges of communication following a fallout, to once again attain that lost harmony and peace.

8.1. The Aftermath and Acknowledgement

Once the dust of the conflict has settled, the first step towards the recovery is identifying, understanding, and acknowledging the cause of the miscommunication. Digging straight into the heart of the problem may seem daunting, but the journey of understanding must commence from there. Be it a lapse of understanding, a moment of unwarranted anger, or a trail of unspoken words that led to the rift, it is fundamental to identify the root. Each party needs to be honest with themselves first before they can begin to mend fences with their partner.

8.2. The Insightful Introspection

Next, let's engage in some insightful introspection. As the famous saying goes, 'It takes two to tango', this is true for commotion communications too. It's easy to point fingers and assign blame, but in doing so, we often overlook our own role in the dispute.

Using an empathetic lens to review the entire episode can lead to discoveries about your own actions and reactions. These can be blind spots in communication, triggers that you never knew existed, or an entirely different perspective of looking at the same situation. Remember, the idea is not to dwell on the past but to learn from it.

8.3. The Art of Apologizing

An apology, when made with sincerity, can mend the most significant fallouts. It serves as a healing balm on the otherwise bruised relationship. When you apologize, make sure it comes from a genuine place of remorse and not from the obligation to pacify the situation. Genuine apologies bear the power to rebuild the shattered trust and bring the relationship back on track.

But remember, while an apology is a good beginning, it's just that—a beginning. The real work of rebuilding comes after.

8.4. Understanding Emotional Needs

Each one of us, semi-consciously or unconsciously, carries a set of emotional needs that we seek to fulfill in our relationships. It becomes crucial to understand and acknowledge your partner's emotional needs.

It could be the need for space, appreciation, approval, or a blend of these. Understanding these can significantly amplify our efforts towards effective communication and in rebuilding the burnt bridges.

8.5. The Road to Resolution

The resolution may not come quickly, but it will come eventually if you tread on this path with persistence and patience. Bring into use the insights that you have gathered from this journey—about the cause and your role in it, the importance of a genuine apology, and the unmet emotional needs of your partner—and undertake a sincere, open, and patient discussion with your partner.

Engage in a dialogue, not an argument, by using "I' statements rather than "You" statements. For example, rather than saying, "You make me feel unheard," convey, "I feel unheard when..." This helps prevent defensiveness and encourages a fruitful conversation.

This process isn't only about rebuilding lost connections; it's also about fortifying your relationship against future communication troubles. As you embark upon this journey, remember that the key is to stay patient and positive. It might not be the fastest journey, but it indeed is the most rewarding. So, here's to breaking barriers and building bridges, one step at a time.

Chapter 9. The Triad of Appreciation, Respect and Empathy: Foundations of Healthy Communication

In the quest for effective communication, three concepts continually circle the nucleus of every successful relationship: Appreciation, Respect, and Empathy. They form the fundamental building blocks for relationship prosperity, nurturing acceptance, understanding, and genuine care. Let's delve deeper to understand the roles they play and how we can foster their growth in our relationships.

9.1. Appreciation: The Connective Fabric

Appreciation, often viewed as the magic bullet, serves as the connective tissue in the relationship. Little drops of gratitude, like morning dew on the leaves, can foster respect, love, and understanding, creating a rich soil for the relationship to bloom.

Appreciation manifests itself in various forms across dimensions of a relationship. In a busy world where we continually juggle multiple obligations, taking a brief moment to acknowledge your partner's efforts can set the tone for constructive communication. This warm recognition fuels the desire in partners to work together, solving problems, and growing the relationship.

To harness the power of appreciation, start by observing your partner more closely. Identify the efforts they put into the relationship. Maybe they take out trash without being asked, or cook your favorite meal when you're stressed. Acknowledge these acts with verbal or non-verbal cues. Let your partner know they're seen, and their actions, however small, are valued.

9.2. Respect: The Cogwheel of Reciprocity

Respect serves as a cornerstone in fostering and maintaining healthy communication. Viewing your partner as an equal is crucial; only then can their perspective be acknowledged and understood. Respect also entails honoring your partner's individuality and their right to hold different beliefs, opinions or preferences.

Respect isn't merely limited to grand gestures. It's as simple as listening mindfully when your partner is talking, not interrupting, accepting their decisions, or giving them space when required. Valuing your partner's time and setting mutual boundaries are equally important.

Remember, respect is reciprocal. Carving out a relationship environment where both partners mutually respect each other paves the way for robust communication dynamics. It acknowledges the fact that each partner is a distinct individual with their unique contributions to the relationship.

9.3. Empathy: The Bridge Across Troubled Water

Last, but certainly not least, empathy forms the foundation of establishing a connection at a deeper level. It involves understanding and sharing your partner's emotions and experiences as though they were your own.

Practicing empathy requires attentive effort. Listening is the first step, but true empathy goes beyond just 'hearing'. It's about thoughtfully considering your partner's viewpoint, feelings, and experiences, and reflecting them back in a compassionate manner.

Learn the art of 'empathetic listening'. Hear their words, read their body language, try to understand their emotional state. Respond in a supportive manner, like validating their feelings or offering comforting words. Regular empathy exercises can be beneficial in enhancing this skill.

By developing empathy, you become more attuned to your partner's needs, paving the way to improved understanding and intimacy. When empathy permeates through the relationship, it paves the way to overcome barriers and sustain healthier communication.

9.4. Converging Appreciation, Respect, and Empathy

Although appreciation, respect, and empathy function independently, they converge synergistically to forge a strong bond in your relationship. Like the notes in a grand symphony, they complement each other and deliver a sensual experience as partners constantly express their admiration, honor each other's individuality, and share empathetic understanding.

In turn, these factors are governed by effective communication. It's the vessel that carries these elements between the partners, facilitating their expression and reception.

9.5. Fostering the Triad in your Relationship

Cultivating appreciation, respect, and empathy isn't an overnight process. It requires consistent effort and commitment. But with these steps, you can infuse these elements in your relationship, leading to a more rewarding communication trajectory.

Practice Mindful Recognition: Regularly identify and appreciate the contributions made by your partner. Practice by setting dedicated moments in the day for expressing gratitude.

Maintain Respectful Communication: Engage in communication that respects your partner's individuality. This includes actively listening, respecting boundaries, and acknowledging differences.

Develop Empathetic Listening: Understand your partner's emotional landscape by practicing empathetic listening. Validating their experiences and emotions contributes to better understanding and intimacy.

In conclusion, the triad of Appreciation, Respect, and Empathy creates a fertile ground for effective communication. Nourishing these elements will help you align your communication patterns, understand your partner better, and traverse through the challenging maze of love and relationships with more poise and confidence. The power to break the barriers lies with you, initiate the journey, and witness the transformation in your relationships!

Chapter 10. Maintaining Open Channels: Effective Strategies for Regular Communication

Relationships are complex constructs, governed by layers of human emotions, thoughts, individual ideologies, and a shared perspective on life. One of such essential layers is communication. Without keeping channels of communication open, we risk derailing our most cherished relationships. Here, we're going to delve into strategies to maintain open channels for constant and effective dialogue.

10.1. Understanding the Basics

Consider your relationship as a garden. Just as a garden thrives with regular watering, sunlight, and nutrient-dense soil, relationships need the nurturing of open, honest and regular communication. If one undertakes the vital task of gardening the mind and nurturing the relationship through words and deeds, the results are blossoms of happiness and satisfaction. However, before we deep dive into techniques and strategies, it is crucial to understand a few basics.

The first step is recognizing the essence of effective communication, which revolves around clarity, consistency, honesty, and empathy.

It's also equally important to understand that communication does not mean talking alone. It is a two-way process that involves listening as earnestly as speaking. And beyond verbal talk, non-verbal cues play a crucial role in deciphering the deeper feelings and emotions. Eye Contact, body language, and tone are vital non-verbal aspects of effective communication.

10.2. Embrace Vulnerability

When you allow yourself to be vulnerable, it opens up a profound passage for honest conversation. Accepting vulnerability and permitting yourself to open up may seem daunting, but it cultivates an environment of trust, authenticity, and acceptance. Start with sharing your feelings, your fears, and your joys. This not only makes you approachable but also helps you connect deeply with your partner.

10.3. Regular Discussions

The simplest way to maintain open communication lines is to ensure you set time for regular discussions. This does not mean you must have some complex, profound dialogue every day. Instead, habitualise discussing your everyday activities, share your thoughts about random things, your views on news or events. This fosters a culture of constant communication, and over time, it becomes second nature.

Remember, the intention is not to create an avenue for debating or arguing. The aim is to cultivate an environment where both parties feel safe to express, listen, and understand.

10.4. Listening

Active listening is as important, if not more, than effective speaking. It is a sign of respect and interest in what the other person is saying. Don't just hear the words; understand the emotions behind them; listen to their body language; observe the unsaid symbolism in their speech. Recognize their joys, apprehensions, concerns, and empathize with their situations.

10.5. Non-verbal Communication

The crucial yet easily neglected part of communication is non-verbal cues. You convey much more through your body language, gaze, and tone than the words you speak. Be conscious of this form of communication. For example, make sure your body language is open when you're in a conversation. Crossed arms often send a signal of defensive or closed off behaviour, potentially hindering open communication.

10.6. Constructive Criticism

In relationships, criticism is unavoidable. However, there is a difference between constructive criticism and outright negative criticism. The former is about presenting the points of improvement while acknowledging the positives. The latter might solely focus on faults, often leading to defensiveness or argument. Constructive criticism when done right, can improve communication and deepen trust in a relationship.

10.7. Emotional Transparency

A strong pillar of open communication is the transparency of feelings. It requires courage, comfort, and trust. By sharing your emotions, you become an open book to your partner. This forms an emotional bond and builds a foundation for robust dialogue.

10.8. Patience and Perseverance

Evolution of communication channels doesn't happen overnight. There may be setbacks, frustration, and arguments. The key here is to be patient with the process and perseverance in making efforts. It's okay to fall, but it is important to rise again and strive for improvement.

In synopsis, communication is a lifelong skill, not a day's task. From understanding the basics to cultivating emotional transparency, every aspect mentioned here requires consistent practice. Always remember - no two people are entirely alike. Differences will exist. However, it's how these differences are communicated, understood, and accepted that define the strength of a relationship. Thus, practicing these strategies can significantly contribute to maintaining open channels of communication, leading to a fulfilling and enriching relationship experience.

Chapter 11. Journey Beyond Words: Creating a Sustainable Communication Environment

Love and understanding can easily get lost in the maze of words. It is within this complex nexus of verbal and non-verbal cues that we often misinterpret, miscommunicate, and inconvenience one another, leading to discontentment and fractures in relationships. But fear not, for the purpose of this chapter is to guide you towards creating a sustainable communication environment in your relationships, a journey that goes beyond mere words.

11.1. Opening Up

Breaking down the walls and opening up may sound simple, but it is often the most challenging part of establishing healthy communication. Honesty is essential, yet we refuse to lower our guards due to fear of being judged, getting hurt, or facing unpleasant reactions.

So how do we begin? The start point is self-awareness. Recognize your fears, desires, and expectations. It's not about exposing weaknesses, rather, it's about acknowledging all aspects of your personality. As you understand yourself better, it becomes easier to communicate your thoughts and feelings to your partner.

11.2. Active Listening

Communication isn't just about expressing, it's equally about understanding. Active listening is a crucial factor in achieving this. It involves full attention to the speaker, refraining from interrupting, and taking the time to understand, empathize, and respond.

Active listening isn't about agreeing with everything your partner says. Instead, it's about valuing their opinion, even when it differs from yours. It's about making them feel heard and giving them the space to express without fear of retaliation or dismissiveness.

11.3. The Power of Patience

While we are adept at quick problem-solving in many aspects of life, a relationship requires patience. Communicating in a relationship is not a competition to be right, but a collaboration to understand.

Quick judgments, fast conclusions, and impulsive retorts often do more harm than good. Patience means acknowledging that the impact of words can be lasting and profound, hence the need to take the time to think before you speak and respond.

11.4. Non-Verbal Cues

Communication is more than words; it often thrives in silence. Non-verbal cues like body language, eye contact, and touch can speak volumes about one's feelings and intentions. Understanding and decoding these silent expressions can significantly enhance your communication effectiveness.

Be mindful of your partner's non-verbal cues. They could be communicating without uttering a single word. Recognizing and responding to non-verbal cues can create depth and richness in your conversations.

11.5. Removing Distortions

Just as a distorted signal can disrupt a call, mental and emotional distortions can disrupt communication in a relationship. Jealousy, worry, insecurities, past conflicts, and grudges are some common distortion-causing elements.

Dealing with such distortions requires mindfulness and effort. Genuine efforts to free your communication from such distortions will result in clearer, more effective exchanges between you and your partner.

11.6. Building Respect

Respect is an essential ingredient in all forms of communication, and it is no different in relationships. Regardless of disagreements and differences in viewpoints, each person deserves to express their feelings without fear of disparagement.

Respect promotes a free flow of ideas and emotions resulting in a much healthier communication environment. It acts as a buffer, protecting the relationship from damaging conflicts and misunderstandings.

11.7. Continuous Learning

Love based on understanding is not a destination; it's a continuous journey. It requires constant learning, unlearning, and relearning. The same applies to communication in a relationship. What worked yesterday may not work today, and what works today may not work tomorrow.

Accept that adjusting your communication style will be an ongoing process. Being open to change and adapting to new strategies will ensure that your relationship is always growing.

While it may seem daunting at first, the journey beyond words helps replace chaos and confusion with clarity and compassion. So fret not, for you're not alone in this. One word, one step at a time, and you're on your way to creating a sustainable communication environment, breeding love, respect, understanding, and togetherness. Let's keep the conversations going, and the love flowing!